DRIFTED

For all of us, "strangers and pilgrims" in a strange land (1 Pet. 2:11), life is an adventurous journey fraught with many missteps and misadventures, we can be certain that the only reliable road map is the Word of God, the Holy Bible. We are most blessed if somehow we find our way to it and embrace it as our very own personal lifeline, a lamp unto our feet. Shevon Frederick has indeed found her way to this ultimate road map.

Drifted shows her how perilous the journey can be without Christ and how very profitable a life well lived with Christ can be. Shevon's inspiring story of courage and determination to seek the Lord's will and purpose for her life despite the ever-present temptations of the flesh is a study of spiritual victory and a testament to her strong character.

The writer's picture of her early life in Trinidad educates us and offers great insight into a lifestyle other than our American way of life yet astutely blends the similarities of the two cultures together into a harmonious whole.

Shevon is a beautiful vessel in the hands of a just and loving God. Her book is an honest testimony to the convictions she holds. Unabashedly she shows us her human side, which reveals the human condition of all of us.

I thoroughly enjoyed her story and heartily endorse her wonderful new book, *Drifted*, which I hope will touch and bless everyone who reads it. As Shevon has poured out her heart and soul to us, perhaps we will find the freedom of release to do the same, emulating her courageous effort. I am honored to have the opportunity to endorse this great work.

—GERALDINE L. HARRIS
RETIRED TEACHER
EDITOR AND AUTHOR

DRIFTED

Shevon Frederick

DRIFTED by Shevon Frederick
Published by Creation House
A Charisma Media Company
600 Rinehart Road
Lake Mary, Florida 32746
www.charismamedia.com

This book or parts thereof may not be reproduced in any form, stored in a retrieval system, or transmitted in any form by any means—electronic, mechanical, photocopy, recording, or otherwise—without prior written permission of the publisher, except as provided by United States of America copyright law.

The names in this text have been changed. Any resemblance to actual people, whether living or dead, is coincidental.

Unless otherwise noted, all Scripture quotations are from the King James Version of the Bible.

Scripture quotations marked AMP are from the Amplified Bible. Old Testament copyright © 1965, 1987 by the Zondervan Corporation. The Amplified New Testament copyright © 1954, 1958, 1987 by the Lockman Foundation. Used by permission.

Scripture quotations marked NKJV are from the New King James Version of the Bible. Copyright © 1979, 1980, 1982 by Thomas Nelson, Inc., publishers. Used by permission.

Scripture quotations marked TLB are from The Living Bible. Copyright © 1971. Used by permission of Tyndale House Publishers, Inc., Wheaton, IL 60189. All rights reserved.

Design Director: Bill Johnson
Cover design by Nathan Morgan

Copyright © 2011 by Shevon Frederick
All rights reserved

Visit the author's website: www.shevonfrederick.com

Library of Congress Cataloging-in-Publication Data:
2011928566
International Standard Book Number: 978-1-61638-609-2

While the author has made every effort to provide accurate telephone numbers and Internet addresses at the time of publication, neither the publisher nor the author assumes any responsibility for errors or for changes that occur after publication.

First edition

11 12 13 14 15 — 987654321
Printed in Canada

DEDICATION

I wish to dedicate this book to almighty God, Who knew my true path before the Earth's foundation. Praise His holy name.

To Jesus Christ, Who remains Mediator and Savior of my soul. Hallelujah!

To the blessed Holy Spirit, Who has brought clarification to this venture and has given me the unction to function through adversity.

SPECIAL THANKS

To my relatives and friends who cared for or assisted my wards during my absence from their lives: You were part of God's divine plan.

ACKNOWLEDGMENTS

There are a few people who supported me through their kind words, moral support, or sheer interest in any work I penned.

I therefore extend my gratitude to Pastor E. Sampson, who believed the Lord spoke to me over a decade ago.

To Denise E. Matthews, who took time from her busy schedule to render her typing skills during the wee hours of the morning.

To Pastor Irving Celestine, who interceded on my behalf during my fragile moments.

To Mrs. E. Dianne Rivera, who encouraged her workers to gain as much knowledge in education as possible.

To Carol-Ann Caliszuski, who is desirous of seeing my writing dreams come true.

Finally, thank you to all my friends, my brother and his wife, Reverend Woods, and the Creation House team for any assistance rendered.

CONTENTS

Introduction 1
1. Transparency 3
2. Transformation 9
3. Repeated Failure 15
4. Camping 19
5. The Effectiveness of Youth Groups 23
6. Added Responsibilities 27
7. My Travels 33
8. Another Side of Christianity 37
9. Obtaining Custody 41
10. Infatuation 47
11. Destructive Paths 51
12. Casting My Cares 55
13. Rebuked by God's Words 59
14. Bearing Another's Burdens 63
15. Moving Forward 67
16. Decisions 71
17. Paying a Price 79
18. Christian Girl Talk 81
19. An Old Policy 87
20. Fact-Finding Mission 91
21. One Final Thought 95
    About the Author 97
    Contact the Author 98

INTRODUCTION

WHENEVER ALMIGHTY GOD speaks, one becomes immediately filled with elation. Inwardly, the individual longs for clarity, as I have. If God says change will come shortly, thoughts quickly run through the mind: *Maybe it's marriage the Lord is referring to—maybe it's death or separation.* Over time, we learn that "change" might simply refer to a minor adjustment, or it could refer to a major transition such as migration or adoption.

The importance of God's Word in our lives is virtually depicted because we all must deal with change. This, however, does not pertain only to the memorization of scripture verses but also to hearing His voice while serving in His presence. Sometimes responsibilities are thrust upon us, and we murmur and complain. We can alter our old lifestyles, and we can also adopt new life principles from this generation. Learn how, when, and why a man-made responsibility ultimately became a God-given opportunity for me within these chapters.

If it were a matter of mere boasting, the information in my book about my travels would have been eliminated; however, young Christians need to know that Christianity is not confined to the walls that surround us on Sundays. Read how the children of my era progressed and adapted with the passage of time.

Love or infatuation will one day greet us all at the door. It may mean joy for some, it may mean pleasure for others, or it may mean all-around disappointment. In the pages that follow, the writer will expose you to the number of platters on which the love was presented during her lifetime.

Initially I held the view that some sinful behaviors existed only in people from the non-Christian community, but the Lord has released to me a number of revelations that have caused me to reconsider. Some light is shown on the naivety that exists in our congregations, among both young and old people. *Drifted* was birthed from own mistakes and sins, and I hope that it will bring readers clarity on several issues.

Finally, I believe that God speaks to each of us in many ways. I hope that *Drifted* enables you to become more sensitive to His value. "Now," according to 1 Thessalonians 5:23, "may the God of peace Himself sanctify [me] completely; and may [my] whole spirit, soul, and body be preserved blameless at the coming of our Lord Jesus Christ!" (NKJV)

Chapter 1

TRANSPARENCY

I HAD SINNED AGAINST almighty God. I approached Him in prayer because I lacked the comfort and luxury of addressing my sin with my local church. Therefore, I launched my complaint to God.

"I was not looking for a boyfriend," I complained. "I was perfectly alright until You allowed these children into my life. I should have had children of my own, and the burden would have become bearable." I was furious with myself. I expressed indignation. I was angry with everyone who was privy to my sin.

In my estimation, sin stems from the verbalization of certain words, an initiated thought, or flurry of emotions. Consequently, I complained to my heavenly Father about them, and His response was, "Write about it." Not in so many words, but it gnawed at my spirit. I continued to argue with God, saying, "But isn't that vindictiveness?"

Some time later at an altar call, my need to write about my past was partially confirmed by a prayerful woman at my former assembly.

Meanwhile, there seemed to be an idea for another book tugging at my spirit, so I attempted to write it. I cannot say that all of its contents or its title had met the approval of its True Owner; therefore, I rarely discuss it.

As time progressed, I began to see the enemy infiltrating the believers' territories with his wicked devices. He works in subtle ways that are no different from those with which he deceived Adam and Eve. Remember the scripture verse about the temptation, "You shall not surely die" (Gen. 3:4, AMP).

Burdened to inform victims of knowledge to which they might not be privy, I had written another script, "Fallen for the Unbeliever." In it, I had sensitized ministers, parents, teenagers, and singles to reasons why we might be failing in some aspects of Christianity, or as a church.

Nevertheless, several years elapsed and one of my biggest fears stared me straight in the face: once again, I had committed a moral failure—I had indulged in an inappropriate behavior. Over the years, however, I have found that I must personalize, not generalize, my behavior, and embrace transparency.

I am the last child of my parents, Stanley C. Frederick and Cynthia E. Frederick, born and raised in the flourishing southern borough of Point Fortin on the island of Trinidad, from the twin island state, the Republic of Trinidad and Tobago.

Trinidad is one of the southernmost isles in the Eastern Caribbean, where a mere forty minutes by air takes us into neighboring Venezuela. According to the U.S. Department of State, its population carries approximately 1.2 million people, and its chief resource is petroleum. Although asphalt gains little recognition, in reality it is the black gold that Trinidad is famous for exporting to Europe.

Nevertheless, because not everyone can gain employment in the oil industry, we are privileged to embrace the Iron and Steel Company of Trinidad and Tobago and the Atlantic Liquefied Natural Gas Company of Trinidad and Tobago, to name a few.

My parents' house was erected in the oil-riddled town of Point Fortin. Most of what I was acquainted with as a child has vanished, with the exception of Trinmar Oil Company. Dunlop Tyre Company, a prominent company, has also disappeared, and many of the schools are also different.

At one time, the town of Point Fortin was filled with pumping jacks, oilrigs, and gigantic silver storage tanks. Today, some of these are no longer in existence, though some oil rigs like Halliburton's are seen on location. Shell and British Oil, now Petrotrin, now operate in other parts of the country but not in "Point."

Even though Trinidad was able to loan neighboring islands millions of dollars in the 1970s, the village in which I was raised is still developing, and still seems a tad neglected. Decades have come and gone, and some streets still face an infrequent or interrupted water supply. The government has changed hands repeatedly. While some folks in my hometown are doing remarkably well, many are still in need of assistance. Also, to this day, most of us still need answers.

The village obviously celebrated more religious activities than any other village in the Borough. This manifested itself through the occasional late-night African drummers and dancers. Additionally, the struggle to comprehend the difference between the practice of Hinduism as opposed to that of the Muslim religion was another factor.

My parents were not wealthy people, but my father was a good provider, so I never felt like a poor person. He worked as a builder of hospitals, schools, and other governmental institutions in the construction industry at Wimpey Construction Firm. Though he earned a good salary with that company, he eventually became a famous contractor, modifying homes at Techier Village, which the British folks had erected.

Some of my older siblings may have experienced some measure of lack when they were growing up, but I did not. Father allowed us to credit items at the nearby Chinese grocery store, and every week he would clear the bill, making it impossible for us to go hungry. Furthermore, although poverty and drugs usually strolled hand in hand when I was growing up, Father and Mother were both overly strict people who exercised strictness to prevent our indulgence.

My parents were not the only ones who supported me financially. I must have been eight or nine years of age when my oldest sister, Nora, sent me about seventeen dresses just adequate for church. Other informal wear was included too, since Nora had already emigrated to U.S. territory.

Whenever my parents and sister did not provide for my well being, my godmother would purchase gifts and fill any financial lack that I might have suffered. As I reminisce, I can still recall the Christmas season when Godmother took me shopping for shoes and gifts. Then we went grocery shopping before returning home, and that just made my day. She was gainfully employed at a local bank. She was still single and childless, so she spoiled me. They all spoiled me.

During my childhood to young adult life, I wore thick, shoulder-length hair. I was a chubby child, and the youngest of my three brothers gave me a nickname as a result, which I simply chose to forget. There was also a tad of tomboy in me.

Mother was a stay-at-home mom, and she indulged

in a good deal of track-and-field and cricket events. She conducted most days as if my siblings and I were live in concert. Two of my older sisters were talented singers who later became members of the Roman Catholic Folk Choir and Christmas Chorale, respectively. Mother, too, was a lead voice at their senior choir, but I never indulged, as my voice was too undeveloped. However, my brothers and I found artistic relief in poetry. We would take turns reciting "The Sands O' Dee" by Charles Kingsley, and other poetry with which Mother and the boys were acquainted.

    I later entered into poetry recitation competitions at the elementary level and performed quite well. Even at church competitions, I often emerged victorious. Mother taught me almost everything I needed to know in order to impact my audience. As I grew older, others from my elementary school and from my local church furnished me with other pointers for success. They all played a vital role in my endeavors and triumphs. All glory goes to the Lord!

Chapter 2

TRANSFORMATION

I WAS BORN INTO Roman Catholicism, and was actually raised in the church until I reached twelve years of age. On a few occasions I attended choir rehearsals with my mom, and I accompanied her at the "Giving of Thanks," a Thanksgiving feast held by many Catholics. Mother was usually either assisting with meal preparation, which she had a knack for, or conducting the Rosary, or "Pass Chaplet," as it was called locally. Mother was a devout Catholic, and as a result, I enjoyed much favor at that parish.

At the age of nine, Sister Elizabeth selected me from my elementary school to take the first communion with some of the Caucasian children from the Clifton Hill Preparatory School, a school designed for the children of the oil field workers. The Clifton Hill area was equipped with bungalows built by the British. Its other accommodations for workers to entertain themselves included a pool, a tennis court facility, a sports club, and a golf course with a seaside hotel.

Before the occurrence of such an undertaking as communion, each child was required to attend confession. Sister Beth would sit us down and explain that each of us had sin operating in our lives. Lying and stealing may not seem sins to young children, but they are. "Even if you took your mommy's milk and sugar, or stole something from your neighbor, you must go to Father and confess your sin."

As I knelt before the priest and labeled my sins, he asked a very strange question. *What did he mean?* I pondered. *Was he asking if I had been insolent to my parents? Or was he referring to sexual abuse among children?*

This terminology was pretty common among children, but how did Father, as priests are generally called, know that? In time, others hinted that they had heard the same wording or expression from him, as well as from another priest.

I was exposed to this type of sexual behavior during child play. Two children in particular played regular games with me, until we drifted elsewhere. The younger of the two girls had exposed me to a basic behavior she had seen exhibited by her parents. Later she affirmed, "It must be done with boys, and it must be a secret. Children who talk too much would get you into trouble." I often wondered whether or not I would have drifted into a homosexual lifestyle if she had said, "It's better with girls!"

Father was oblivious to the new behavior I had acquired. My mother, on the other hand, found out about it somehow, and spanked and lectured me as a result.

At the confessional, I still cannot recall my response. I remember being instructed to go kneel down and say a limited number of Hail Marys and a specified number of Our Fathers. They were supposed to make it all right, while Father interceded on my behalf for my sins.

Years later, Mother severed all ties with the Catholic Church. She accepted Jesus Christ as savior into her heart and felt that she no longer wished to pray to the saints or to Mary; she now considered this to be idol worship, and strongly condemned it. She watched Rex Humbard on television, as she had not yet found a place to worship. She rebuked everyone who came to recapture her interest in the Catholic faith and admitted that she liked the church, but "We [were] doing something wrong. The Catechism," she pointed out, "says we should not bow down to them or serve them. Yet we are doing the very thing." Mother also believed that there were several other areas in which the teaching of the Catechism was seemingly being contradicted by the practice.

During that era, two of my older sisters also gave their hearts to the Lord. They, too, had no desire to return to the Catholic Church. I was now twelve years old and furious that they were willing to disrupt my life. I liked my life as it was; now everything seemed to be unraveling so quickly.

One day, a young girl had passed through our neighborhood while conducting a census. She was a Christian, and fellowshipped at the Pentecostal church in our town. That was it! Mother and the girls agreed that they would begin attending there. When I complained, one of my sisters said, "You can return to the old church if you like. We simply won't be going with you." Nothing negative had happened to them at the old church. They had just found Christ as Savior and Lord, and could not indulge in the previous type of fellowship anymore.

Not having a choice or say in the matter, I followed my family to church every week, Sunday after Sunday. I also attended some of the church's Monday, Tuesday, and Friday night prayer meetings, although I behaved like Lot's wife during this time, always looking back.

Gradually I began paying attention, and also noticed that there were a few kids around my age there. The church was like a chapel in those days. The pastor urged sinners to come to the altar to accept Christ as Savior, and at some point I remember going forward. Not fully comprehending the seriousness of the decision, I joined the class for converts and water baptism, along with my other family members.

They knew exactly what they were doing; I had only a faint idea. Nevertheless, I was immersed in water on the same day as Mother and my two sisters. They rambled about the joy they felt; "the inner peace," they called it. I could not say the same, but I had made a decision and needed to walk or abide in it. Maybe I was too young to comprehend what they felt. I had not displayed any type of rebellion, but within my spirit I felt they had gone too far, especially during the Carnival, or Mardi Gras celebration. There was no need for me to join in the street dance, but I needed my presence to be felt at the festivities.

I was attending secondary school, and other children or students made fun of those who would not participate in the Carnival celebrations. I felt that if I had remained a Catholic, I simply would have needed ashes on my forehead on Ash Wednesday after celebrating Carnival to cleanse my sins, I suppose.

"Carnival camps" are where most Christians spent their quiet time. It was refreshing, and in time I had discovered a new way of life, a new way to live. Camp always involved people from various sister churches or assemblies from other towns. Therefore, my list of friends and acquaintances kept increasing. It was healthy. It was informative. It was spiritual. It was fun. There was much talk about getting filled with the Holy Ghost at the Carnival camp as the disciples had been filled in the Upper Room.

Years later, at the age of fourteen or fifteen, I was in

an all-girl class and gained fresh knowledge. There was a group or clique that was a tad older than me and quite versed in many areas of life. When they spoke, I simply listened. Some suggestions seemed like ones to cherish or hold on to should I require them in the future. Others, I immediately knew within, would be bad for me.

I truly believed the other students when I learned that parties were packed with fun. The others claimed, "you're missing out on the fun by attending church only." When one of my relatives invited me to her daughter's birthday party, I willingly accepted the invitation. Unfortunately, the party was nothing like I had imagined. The invitees were in complete control. They turned the lights off frequently, and the guys held the girls closely in various sections of the room. The body movements and gyrations were not what I had anticipated, or what I desired. I had seen enough; I closed the bedroom door from which I peeked out, and went to sleep. As I began to realize that the things my classmates referred to as "fun" were not fun at all, I knew in my heart that the Lord had truly touched my life.

Due to the seating accommodations in the classroom, I overheard the conversations of many of my classmates. One day, Joan and Beth asked another classmate named Liz if she had started having intercourse yet. When she responded that she had not, they told her—among other things—how much she was missing out on. When Liz did begin having intercourse, she supplied them with all the details of the relationship, and they chuckled constantly.

Many months later, Liz became pregnant. Joan walked from desk to desk asking everyone if they had observed "Lizzy's swollen stomach." "Is she pregnant? Take a good look at *her*." Then she chuckled again. I watched, and observed how they rejoiced to see their friend—just sixteen—pregnant and unmarried. Again, I pondered these things.

Chapter 3

REPEATED FAILURE

P
ORTIA WAS OLDER than me, but we connected beautifully. One evening, after classes had been dismissed for the day, Portia and I headed out the main gate, the lone exit at the front of the school, which was primarily private property. Public transportation was prohibited in that location. No businesses existed or operated there, and what little activity was presented came from an oil refinery or two. Large silver storage tanks flanked both sides of the roadway, and students queued up along the roadway, just meters away from the sea bathing area.

Portia and I continued conversing while threading through this panoramic, expansive site. The vicinity was extremely tranquil and clean, with the exception of the occasional fumes of gasoline, kerosene, or jet fuel gases discharged into the atmosphere. Pipelines connected to the body of large silver tanks combed the area like veins.

In mere minutes, we reached the main office, a colossal building that housed managers and secretaries, and a medical office for the workers at the petroleum companies. In another couple of minutes, we arrived at the main street where we parted with each other until the next school day.

It was during one of those evening walks that we met Ross.

"How are you, Ross?" Portia inquired. "And how's John?"

"John's doing fine," he responded.

She introduced me to Ross, and the two of them continued their conversation. I must have said good-bye at some point, because we all lived in different directions.

Portia and John (who I eventually learned was Ross's brother) were an item, but I was oblivious to this, as my friendship with Portia was relatively new.

At school the following day, Portia turned toward me with a smile on her face and remarked, "Ross says he likes you."

I asked softly, "And who is Ross?"

"The guy I was speaking with yesterday. He is John's brother." She declared.

"And who is John?" I insisted.

"John is my boyfriend," she confirmed.

The next encounter we had with Ross was a very pleasant one. He spoke with me and asked me my name again. He told me his, and asked whether I had brothers and sisters. I answered yes. When he repeated his last name, I realized that his older brother and one of my older brothers were classmates. As simple as that, our friendship began.

Ross was fair in complexion and very handsome. He was very methodical, and also quite ambitious. He was clever and treated me with kindness. As time progressed, I grew to love Ross completely.

I cannot label our initial encounter a sham. Relationships are never a sham from the onset. Having a normal conversation with another person is never an enjoyment of double-standard principles. Discovering what they are capable of luring us into is where the real problem commences. I can name it naivety on my part, but I certainly was not seeking to be pretensive or to delude anyone, because I was not looking for a boyfriend.

For many months, Ross and I enjoyed healthy, clean, simple conversations. Communication and rapport between us seemed to be pure and genuine. What pure-thinking teenager would envision that something immoral could result in the future?

It started with a birthday kiss. Then, months later, it intensified into what Ross implicitly described as behaviors that couples engage in when they love each other. As Christians, such behavior prevents us from tapping into the flow of the Spirit. Therefore, this situation, along with the fact that Ross was already involved with another teenaged girl, encouraged me to sever ties with him periodically. (I say "periodically" because on about two occasions, Ross and I drifted into an on-again-off-again relationship. Although one guy at the church had displayed a measure of interest in me, the connection between Ross and me was just too profound.)

Chapter 4

CAMPING

IN MY LIFETIME, I have attended more camps than I could have possibly imagined. My involvement in various groups has afforded me many privileges. They were meant to be fun-filled adventures, and I did have an incredible amount of fun. My first camp was held at Los Iros Beach facilities. I can vaguely recall some of the events that unfolded while we camped with members from two other Pentecostal Churches.

We were all southern churches, but our exposure with the Word was of vast difference. One could easily pinpoint the learned from the unlearned among us, the talented from the amateurs, and the Spirit-filled ones from those who simply beat the air.

I was only a child then, and so many memories of the events have gradually faded. I remember that there was a time for sea bathing, but after the sea claimed a life, we were prohibited from entering the waters. I also remember that I gained a friend during that time, and I visited her hometown about a year later, a former historic site with predominantly Spanish descendants. I recall hearing various stories–fables that I no longer entertain–of street parades and the sighting of a Saint, La Divina Pastora, emanating from that town on the local news.

As I became older, I attended my first ISCF camp. Because it was named Inner Schools Christian Fellowship, we were permitted to camp at various public schools. The fellowship later purchased its own campsite.

The highlight of the IS camp was banquet night. Everyone drew a slip of paper or chit with someone else's name on it from a box. We were then allowed to dine with the boy who picked our name (there was lots of adult supervision). There was entertainment and a display of etiquette or decorum. There was no voraciousness displayed. It was purely a fun-filled event, as was the entire camp.

I did attend one more IS camp, which was also filled with excitement and entertainment. Campfire was the highlight of that camp. Later, tadpoles were slipped through the windows of one or two dormitories, and campers were mushed, or smeared with powder or ketchup as they walked down the corridors. Again, each of these pranks was executed in good taste. These events climaxed the night before each camper's bags were packed to return home. I would never see many of those faces ever again—at least not in this lifetime.

The Cowen Hamilton Camp was different because we were all teenagers coming from different educational backgrounds. There were the extremely brilliant ones, who attended schools that only admit the most gifted students, and there were those of us who were just good students in the system.

Chapel was interesting, but the tremendous spiritual emphasis that was placed on other camps—like Christian education, youth ministries, or even Crusaders Camps—was non-existent. We had chapel and lectures, but there was no Upper Room experience or Holy Ghost-filled night for which the Christian young adult camps were famous.

Camping

It was Carnival, or Mardi Gras, time again. I had the option to remain at home and view the proceedings on television, or I could attend camp. Once again, I chose to attend camp. Carnival camp on the mountain was memorable, especially the hike to the pinnacle of the mountain, which stood out in everyone's mind. Upon returning to the campsite, most campers gave testimonies of the difficulty of the exercise, all indicating that the experience was very much like Christianity. Some complained that it was extremely difficult to reach the top, and consequently returned to the campsite.

Everyone traveled blindly, unaware of the distance and height we were required to reach. The pine-tree leaves on the ground added to the difficulty of the hike; we would reach a certain height and slide downward again. When improper footwear or attire was worn, the difficulty of such an undertaking was intensified. Many of us grabbed onto shrubs or vines to help us reach the summit.

A firm mind-set was obviously needed in order to reach the top. Some folks were far ahead of the line, which helped to encourage and heighten our aspirations, giving us the incentive or assurance we needed to believe that it was safe to continue along the path.

At times, the hill stood straight ahead with no leaves, no curves, and no stones, just a straight, steep hill. Most of us did make it to the end, where we found a shrine, and flat, grassy land spread straight ahead. The valley below housed the West Indies School of Theology, which its students were more than thrilled to brag about.

Yet, this was not my final camp. I was still a young adult when I attended Crusaders Camp, a group originating in Canada with branches operating in some Caribbean countries. Camp was packed with crafts, games, lectures, discussions, the Upper Room experience, a talent search, and, of course, chapel.

The female campers occupied the upper level of the beach house facility, while the boys were housed in the lower level. Everyone was expected to volunteer their services.

Because we were a semi-military Christian-based organization, drills or exercises were conducted during the morning period. Upon completion, a game of "Spirit Is Moving" or "Sing Family" was incorporated. Whether the game of earthlings and angels was taught then, I have no recollection, but it was a carefully executed camp.

Finally, what stands out most in my mind is the lecture or discussion that was conducted for everyone, although I have forgotten most of what was taught on that day. The girls assembled outdoors, and the boys went to another location. I was seated in the back row with friends, when the lecturer stated that petting is a sin. My friend and I turned toward each other and asked, "What is petting?" No one answered the question then, and I cannot recall if we ever got a response. I did not check a dictionary for its true meaning when I arrived home days later.

Chapter 5

THE EFFECTIVENESS OF YOUTH GROUPS

MY MINISTER OFTEN reminded the congregation that our duty as believers was to "be strong in the Lord, and in the power of his might" (Eph. 6:10).

I will try to recapture the moments in which I was at my strongest; as a young believer I ponder on moments in which my involvement in Crusaders, a semi-military church group almost like Girls Guides or the Boy Scouts Association, was effective.

The honor codes served as an inspiration and became a driving force to stability in my early Christian life. Words like the following were uttered at weekly meetings:

- "On my honor, I will guard my heart against disloyalty." A Crusader is loyal to God to his country, his parents, his church, and all Crusaders.

- "On my honor, I will guard my actions against unkindness." A Crusader is kind.

- "I promise to be loyal to God, to my country, my church, and to all Crusaders, and to keep the honor code."

This final promise was the most important in my opinion, and probably kept one from consummating a union before marriage. If I chose to step out of line, one of the ten honor codes propelled me right back into a position of right standing with God, because the semi-military group was also religious.

Does this mean that the Word of God was ineffective in my endeavors? Certainly not! The local church offered its blend of youth rallies during the 1970s and 1980s, taking the form of youth competitions in public speaking and singing individual and group songs. The quizzing department took precedence among the young adults. A book was chosen from the Bible, and usually three chapters were memorized or studied to the best of the quizzers' abilities. I recall there being deductions of points and team questions involved, but a good deal of information has faded with the passage of time. When I chose to participate in one year's Youth Week culmination activities, the first three chapters of the Book of Daniel were selected.

Participants were expected to finish the leader's quotation. For example, the leader would begin quoting Daniel 1:8, "But Daniel purposed..." The contestant from either of the two teams who felt the most confident would jump to his feet and quote the remainder of the scripture: "But Daniel purposed in his heart that he would not defile himself with the portion of the king's meat, nor with the wine which he drank: therefore, he requested of the prince of the eunuchs that he might not defile himself."

Another question read, "What were the names given to the three Hebrew boys?" Quizzers or team captains would then answer, "Hananiah, Michael, and Azariah." Other questions and many other quotations were uttered from the Book of Daniel, and although I was not one of the better quizzers, the study impacted my life in a realistic way.

I became interested when one of my older sisters participated in the study of the Book of Romans chapters 6, 7, and 8. I would memorize her verses as she practiced at home. Although it might seem that the words of Romans 6:1-2, "What shall we say then? Shall we continue in sin, that grace may abound? God forbid," would have very little meaning to me, this scripture has resonated in my heart and mind for so many years, and has served me quite well in times of decision.

Later, sports and track-and-field events took precedent in the church. They help build unity and camaraderie among believers, but equilibrium in the body remains imperative. Whenever there is too much emphasis on "entertainment" in our churches, there is nothing to sustain believers whenever perilous times arise.

However, if the church is fixated upon spiritual things only, people–young people in particular–who are not fully committed may wander. Therefore, I repeat, we need to strike a balance.

Chapter 6

ADDED RESPONSIBILITIES

ENTERING INTO WOMANHOOD created a whole new environment for me. Turning twenty meant new dreams, new visions, and a time to find true meaning and purpose for my life and future.

During this time, my cousin approached my parents, asking them if her daughter could live with us—for a while, at least. I was the only child still living at home at the time, as my older siblings were either married, had emigrated, worked in another town, or traveled abroad on a regular basis. I immediately encouraged father to allow the young child to live with us, as I was not ready to be married at twenty, and life at home was seemingly dull and boring.

Father was overly generous by nature and had assisted others in the past. Mother, too, had her generous moments. They both agreed, as this was a family member—a relative—crying out for assistance.

Rhonda was six years old when she arrived, and already displayed a strong level of intelligence. The responsibility was awesome, but Father felt a sense of duty or obligation because she was Mother's extended family. He addressed the child's fundamental needs. Books and uniforms for school, as well as clothing and shoes for church became entirely Father's responsibility. He also took it upon himself to purchase any items that my cousin Rhonda's school required.

Mother cooked for us, because she enjoyed cooking. She was also an excellent baker, and her grandparents ran a family-owned bakery. I assumed the role of big sister and assisted Rhonda with her homework. I had her laundry done and addressed other menial tasks. I guided her as best as I could.

For two full years the responsibility of raising the young child rested wholly on my own parents. Rhonda attended church services with us and she accompanied me whenever I visited friends. She was now a part of the family, and she seemed to enjoy it. Would she adhere to the rules of our family as she grew older? Would she conform to godly principles? These were never my thoughts, never my concern.

It was about that time that my Asian friend and I contemplated starting the Early Childhood Center, and we succeeded at accomplishing it.

At one point shortly after, my father took a vacation to the United States. It was not until later that I realized that the Lord was stabilizing me during Father's absence, as I had assumed his role while he was gone. The challenge was much greater than I had anticipated. Father and I had traveled to Grenada earlier that very year. I had signed all his travelers' cheques, and that created an awesome feeling within me. But the harsh reality of parenting—of life—had not set in until I was required to address Rhonda's needs entirely by myself. I wanted so badly to embrace parenting as well as he did.

During that time, Rhonda's school had embarked upon a fundraising venture, and I stood in proxy for my dad. My nephew had also come to live with us during

Added Responsibilities

Father's absence. He was only two years old, and while his own father was solely responsible for his financial needs, Mother and I addressed nearly everything else.

Meanwhile, Father's visit was cut short when he became very ill with heart troubles and diabetes, and needed to return home. The strong, tall man, who always walked most erect, swaying his arms from side to side like a soldier, had suddenly succumbed to a mild stroke, in addition to the heart troubles and diabetes that he suffered. He could no longer move as quickly as he once did. In fact, he was required to stay in bed and exercise as much and as often as he could. Mother was dedicated to caring for him. She prepared his meals, assisted him with baths, and dressed him. She became his personal aide. I administered his insulin shots and tests each day. Gradually, his health and condition began to improve. He began walking again with the assistance of his walker and my brothers enabled him to keep his doctor's appointments.

School was already in progress during that period, so I would get his tests completed and rush off to school. And, yes, the kids were still small and needed attention as well. Mother and I rallied around everybody.

I cannot tell what series of events had unfolded when Ross dropped by to say hello. Father met him for the first time, though he had been introduced to Mother some time before. He chatted with Father for a while, and I was sure Father had interrogated him. No one slips by that easily, not with Father–not unless he liked something in you. Nevertheless, they both appeared calm throughout the conversation.

Ross had visited before, in Father's absence. We had addressed serious issues, such as marriage and family, regular topics that couples engaged in. Nevertheless, the time had come and the person most prepared was Ava, Ross's significant other. They married each other and he moved on.

It was just about Christmastime when Ross and I stumbled upon each other at a store. He spoke about a dream he had. He said, "I saw you giving or serving food to people and think you should probably keep a thanksgiving feast at your school." Thanksgiving feast in Trinidad is a time where lots of children and adults come together at any given time to of the year, to give thanks to God for financial blessings bestowed upon them. Ross was always giving me this kind of advice, which he deemed necessary. I cannot remember what my response was, but I do remember that we were always civil to each other.

It was barely weeks later when a time of serving others did come. Father suffered a fatal heart attack just as the new year began. On the morning of the eighth day of the new year, his grandchildren had just returned to the United States after vacationing for Christmas. We had to plan a quick burial in order to accommodate another daughter who needed to return back to the United States in a matter of days.

At the funeral, the church was packed to capacity. Even the churchyard was filled. People passing by may have wondered if this was the funeral of a celebrity or dignitary of some kind. His soul, however, was what mattered most. We know for certain that he is resting in Jesus, because he spoke constantly about his death. Father often said, "don't go too far, should something happen," and "they're coming to take the debris." The funeral agent really did come for his remains, his body, because he died from pulmonary cardiac arrest one Friday morning. Was it a premonition he experienced, or was he just rambling when he talked about climbing a mountain? We did not comprehend the parables of which he spoke, but he was preparing both himself and us. He knew he would meet his maker, Jesus Christ, either as Savior or Judge at his resurrection (Rev. 20:13).

Chapter 7

MY TRAVELS

THE TRAVELS DID not cease after Father's death; instead, they intensified. A group of Christian friends from my former assembly and I went to Margarita, a neighboring Venezuelan Island. Most of us had acquired some degree of proficiency in Spanish at school. Therefore, each of us tried to jog our memory to retrieve appropriate Spanish words.

We added an *o* to some words even when we were not supposed to. Unsure of the true vocabulary usage, we laughed heartily as we needed to recall days of the week, types of weather, and times of day. Each time we confused *martes* and *miércoles* or did not conjugate the verb properly, we were gleeful. Whether *lunes* meant Sunday or Monday, we were sometimes unsure, and such unpreparedness created more hilarious moments and outbursts among us.

There was also the conversion of money. *One thousand Bs are equivalent to what?* Everyone took out their calculators, and even that created moments of laughter, as some of us had little or no knowledge of what we were doing. The exchange rate at their banks changed continuously, and although I did not understand it then, it was something new to learn.

Ordering meals was another jovial time. "*Croissant con jamón y queso y leche o jugo de naranja,*" which is interpreted, "croissant with ham and cheese and milk or orange juice" was my favorite breakfast order. There was never a dull moment during that trip and there were no buffoons among us.

Devotions were almost the only serious time for us. There were two prayerful guys who enjoyed ministering God's Word to us, so they obliged on most occasions. Each of us shared testimonies on the trip. Almost everything was done in the name of fun, and God was well pleased.

Our purpose for visiting the island was solely for shopping. Clothing was seemingly less expensive than other islands, but its quality left much to be desired. We rummaged through items that we needed badly, or sniffed their perfume, often without even making a single purchase. However, the fragrance in their hair products was most desirable, so one friend purchased those instead.

Still, this was not the only vacation I embarked upon after Father was gone. Mother and I paid a visit to London, where her two brothers, sister, and sister-in-law treated us with kindness and generosity and did everything in their power to make our welcome a splendid and interesting one. Even my sister and her family welcomed us with open arms while vacationing in London.

The day after our arrival, we took the underground trains before going onto the tour bus. We observed the changing of the guards, took a long hard look at Buckingham Palace, traveled under the Thames River, and were awestruck with our surroundings. Some time later we were informed that the late Princess Di and Her Majesty Queen Elizabeth often traveled on the very street that we stayed in Tottenham.

My uncle's Mercedes Benz took us everywhere we

needed to go or where they wished to take us. Visiting Madam Toussaud's Wax Museum was interesting, and our trips to Piccadilly Circus and the Cutty Sark were brilliantly executed. The constant shopping, even traveling on a double-decker passenger bus and double-decker plane to Holland, were all memorable experiences. In fact, the entire trip was pleasantly rewarding.

The island of Trinidad has a sister isle, where only a select few have visited or toured. Tobago is not bordered by land from Trinidad as some countries are. In fact, one must travel by airplane for fifteen to twenty minutes because a mass of sea separates one island from the other.

It is relatively cheap to travel by boat, so most people choose to travel on the Panorama Boat. Vehicles occupy the lowest deck while all other occupants utilize the middle and upper decks, suited with cabins. Seating accommodations were at the very top of the small boat, much like an airplane.

The little boat fascinated me because I had underestimated it externally. I have seen other boats, and there was nothing spectacular about them. This boat was not grand, but I clearly expected less. After my girlfriend and I had completed our tour, I surely recommended it to others. The ship sailed between the hours of 2:00 p.m. and 11:00 p.m., and its passengers disembarked either with or without vehicles. It was simply another learning experience that is forever etched in my memory.

Tobago itself had rough but brilliantly clear, blue waters. The island undoubtedly requires some development, but the Buccoo Reef still exists, and many newlyweds occupy the chain of hotels that grace the seashores.

Chapter 8

ANOTHER SIDE OF CHRISTIANITY

It was a quiet period, and the hush and tranquility were evident throughout the island. My People Incorporated had ended its drama productions, as its director had entered a new place in life. They had once held the country captive with their astounding productions; call it live theatre for Christians. The cheering audience would have paid almost any price to have the show return, but many of the members of the group had found love and were now married with children. Their work was never considered amateur; everyone welcomed it as professionalism at its best. They were home-based for a while, but in time they spread their wings throughout the island. Conversation never ceased among the attendees about the brilliance in which each scene had been executed. The actors, the stage, the performance, were all so captivating–always leaving the audience calling for more. There were melancholic moments to as well as moments of jubilation in each play. The applause continues to ring in my ears for My People Incorporated.

Meanwhile, Margaret Elcock, the founder of Christian Radio & Television Broadcast on the island of Trinidad, said she had prayed for about eight years or so, and consequently, Christian programming was on the air. The country, the island, is now so blessed with Christian music that every artist began acting like family when visiting Trinidad.

Therefore, welcoming foreign artists like Helen Baylor to our shores was an enchanting moment. When the only track she had was played, the audience simply called for more. She was very accommodating as she appeased the crowd with all their favorites. The floor of the National Stadium probably cried out as they all jumped to their feet and danced to the tune "I'm Lifting Up the Name of Jesus!" She did pay another visit with her second album, and the greeting was just as enthusiastic.

I was not well acquainted with one of the new artists' music. In fact I knew the songs, but I didn't know the artist's name. I soon discovered it was Ron Kenoly who graced us with his presence. Teenagers and young adults could not wait to get a close-up view of the man himself. He motioned them to draw closer to him, and that was all they needed—to reach out and touch him as he delivered a fascinating performance at that memorable Saturday concert.

Another artist, Alvin Slaughter, probably had no idea about the type of people he would be entertaining. Spoiled by former artists who graced our shores, the cheering Christian crowd cried for more, more, more! At midnight they still cried out for more songs. He had already shared his testimony. The maddening crowd could do nothing but say, "Thank you for a splendid performance; till we meet again," and he did visit again.

I was not prepared to attend a Kirk Franklin concert. When asked if I had purchased a ticket yet, I remarked, "I'm not spending my money to go 'Stomp' with Kirk Franklin. I'm not sixteen." My cousin Rhonda probably attended that concert. It was some time after that performance that I began listening to his other songs like "My Life Is in Your Hands" and "Catch You When You

Fall." Then I saw him; I saw not only the amusing side of him but that he clearly held hands with our Savior and Lord.

Chapter 9

OBTAINING CUSTODY

A THIRD CHILD WAS sent to live with us almost immediately after my father passed away. I refuse to say that I was thrilled about it. My mother tried desperately to offer a reason to justify her parents' decision or action, but I was infuriated. The demands of the two other children weighed heavily on my shoulders. The parent-teacher conferences were extensive. Whether it was for financial or behavioral reasons, two children were enough. Three children seemed like too many at that stage of my life.

The third child arrived when she was two years old. She was firm in speech, and I made no conversation with her. Mother constantly reminded me that she was just a child. Mother was also raised in her grandparents' home, so she saw no sin in it. Mother did not think it wrong for children to live with their grandparents.

I do not think it entirely wrong either but some children seem to think that grandparents should accept full responsibility of their grandchildren with little or no assistance at times.

People often boast, "It takes a village to raise a child." Well, somebody should have told the village about that, because the villagers did nothing to help me raise those children. The adage is true in some instances, but in others it is totally false. Mother's assistance in raising the kids was always appreciated, and it made the burden more bearable. There were occasions when I desperately wanted others to intervene, and there were times when I became very prideful. I actually behaved like they were my biological children and no one else should judge them or provide for them. I knew deep within that they all had shortcomings. The kids were already struggling with questions such as, "Why are you living in your grandmother's house? Where is your father? Why aren't you living with your mother?" I don't believe it was a hindrance to their learning ability, but I knew that they each had concerns and challenges. More concerns became apparent as they grew older.

If Rhonda wanted to attend camp, and I could not provide the finances she needed, I bluntly refused to have her attend. If a stranger offered to make the payment, I rejected that too. Father had paid for all my camping adventures, so my greatest concern was the pride of addressing it myself. Birthday gifts were acceptable. Handouts were not appreciated; they were prohibited. There was something deep within that said, *It is my responsibility and no one else's.*

If it was not addressed in the same manner as Father's, it did not feel right. If family members provided for them, it was fine. Handouts suggested inadequacy, and that created a horrible feeling within me.

If I had a lack that a family member could not address, I would rather borrow the money and repay it at a later date. Some might call this independence. Sometimes the kids' father or their uncle would be their provider, because there were periods of deficiency as well as sufficiency.

There were moments when Rhonda, Dillon, and Kameel's involvement in athletics did create periods of excitement. There were always sufficient funds to address their needs, and the excitement of their achievements was pleasantly rewarding. The trophies, the medals, and the prizes all brought smiles to our faces. There were periods when their grades or performance at school brought the same sense of pride.

Rhonda was an extremely brilliant student. Once, she was promoted to a higher grade because of her performance and ability. I discovered much later in life that she and I had very similar strengths. Whenever there was a measure of weakness in me, the same was replicated in her. Although I did not birth these children, I saw many similarities in our lives. Not in every aspect, but in a few. Rhonda's performance was enhanced as she grew older, while living with a family friend named Sandi. She was a lawyer, and she understood the realities of life and addressed them in a more realistic way.

Seeing the similarities between Rhonda's life and mine, I enrolled Kameel in another school where I felt she could conquer the math problem that I had experienced as a child. Maybe the school was not the problem, but she conquered math to a greater degree than I did.

What I discovered with all three children, however, is that parenting is not just fun. Children are not toys. The responsibility is awesome, even though all of the children were talented and skillful. If your heart and mind are involved, you may do a brilliant job. If you are only partially responsible and the challenges are awesome, the children may suffer serious lack. Delinquent parents harm their offspring much more than they may fathom.

Every child has flaws, but Dillon needed assistance constantly. He had acquired all types of learned behavior, although some were innate or encoded. It was always a challenge with him. I knew so little about Attention Deficit Hyperactivity Disorder (ADHD). Dillon was definitely an ADHD child, but medication was never administered. I was educated on certain aspects of the condition that highlighted the causes, but I really learned its true title and effects from a television show. By then, it was too late to remedy the situation; he was already a teenager and set in his ways.

I always knew he needed special attention, because he could not—or would not—adjust to the challenges of education. Assuming responsibility for him was tremendous and painful. He constantly made excuses and manipulated many people with his tactics. He was a loving and forgiving child, which probably carried him through life. Was Dillon just an unproductive child? Not really. In fact, he was quite skilled at repairing certain parts of cars by the tender age of ten.

Those were the moments in which I strongly rebuked those who claim, "It takes a village." Where were the villagers? Friends, neighbors, and distant relatives all seemed to laugh at my foolishness as a guardian. Whenever the children's education failed, there was laughter. Whenever their behavior left much to be desired, that, too, was hilarious. Whenever delinquency or deficiency emerged, support was never available. I have seen others extend a helping hand to their best friends, but there was something that made them all stand back and watch my failure at parenting. I did, however, have friends in various circles and knew that help was at the door. My friend Sandi did her best, and another friend, Odette, acted like my sister in various aspects of my life. Kudos to them!

One young man, a family friend, simply lavished Dillon with too much money. Forty dollars for an eight-year-old was totally outrageous. What is a young child to do with such an enormous sum of money? The figure increased as he became older. When the figure becomes unattainable, where should he go next? How would he maintain this lifestyle? Yet it was sheer naivety on the part of this young man. He had no immediate family and earned a good deal of money. He probably did not think through his action thoroughly, and did not consider how it would ultimately affect the young child. I could not satisfy his basic needs with five-dollar bills. He was now acquainted with enormous sums of money, which contributed to my difficulty in parenting him. Yet the stories are just as profound with every child.

My only choice was to sever ties with my wards—for my own sanity. They attended church; the girls were involved, but I needed separation. Three children who constantly aligned themselves with their parents, relatives, or friends prevented me from being in total control of the ship.

I once watched Danielle Steel's *No Greater Love* (which in my opinion had all the makings of James Cameron's *Titanic*), and saw my life unfolding before my eyes. I had become an old woman while caring for these children. Sixteen years of my life had simply slipped away. Would I even want children of my own now, after having suffered such humiliation? I became too fragile to attempt such an undertaking again.

Chapter 10

INFATUATION

It was in rash moments like these, when I was at my most vulnerable point, that I would find love or infatuation, sometimes inside religious circles, sometimes outside of the body of Christ. And there were times when such vulnerability did not exist, and yet the opposite sex was completely drawn to me.

Tim was always properly attired—cuffs neatly folded and pants seamed to the hem. His speech bore no impediments or listlessness, and his kindness and generosity were flawless.

I knew that he served the Lord, but I cannot say whether he loved Him with his whole heart. Nevertheless, Tim demonstrated sufficient interest in me, and I needed to make a decision because despite all the great qualities he possessed, he was a nervous person, and also could not hold down a job.

Considering that example that my own father set, as he was so strong in family matters, I felt that Tim did not fit the profile for good parenting, so I simply released him. We dated for a while, and he was a perfect gentleman. Did he remain jobless? No, not really. Would I become a parent or give birth biologically at this stage in my life? I'm hoping not to.

Dick was a Christian. He was very handsome. He came from money, though he had little to offer. His parents owned a light aircraft and a thriving business, but he was still a student. He understood spiritual life quite well and instructed me about several aspects of spiritual warfare. He attended prayer meetings constantly and enjoyed witnessing to others about Jesus. He enjoyed explaining witnessing techniques to me. The sense of humor he expressed along with ways to reach the lost grasped my attention and enveloped me. He did not just seem to be religious; his love for the Lord was genuine.

We would talk on the phone for hours, sometimes from eleven at night to four o'clock the following morning. Conversations with Dick were always learning experiences. Yet there was something I saw in him that I had recognized in other male friends. It caught my attention; I often wondered, *Are there others with a similar story, or is my situation an isolated one?* I discovered there *was* another woman in his life! Yes, Dick was attracted to someone else!

I encountered Tom after the experience I had with Dick. I was inundated with problems. It was twofold. I had tried literally every approach, every procedure, every scheme I knew, and nothing seemed effective.

Dillon, my nephew, had become an impulsive spender. Once I was alerted when he was having a party with friends. Lectures were useless; corporal punishment was ineffective; prayer seemed monotonous then, and nothing else was working. Dillon needed a reality check. *This is the final straw,* I said to myself. "I may need to enroll you in a boys' facility," I concluded.

I took Dillon to the local police station to be educated about prisoners and possibly view a cell or two in the process. The situation spiraled out of control. The cop felt that he was too young to view such cruel undertakings because prisoners were occupying the cells. He took my home phone number in order to keep abreast of daily occurrences or developments involving the child. Dillon knew that the police officer was checking on his whereabouts, so on one hand the pressure was relieved. On the other hand, it intensified, because Tom, the officer, was using every opportunity he knew to get to me. I was young and naive. I was not entirely gullible, having been around other men. The privilege of calling Tom if something seemed shady with Dillon felt relaxing, but the calls to my house were endless. They were constant, continuous, and often unavoidable.

He offered to be a father figure to the child because he had none of his own. I was biting the bait gradually. We had gone out on one or two dates with the young child, of course, and he had made house visits. Therefore, I did show a bit of interest in his offer.

What was odd was that he visited at nighttime, claiming to be "off duty." The situation was heading in a direction that was uncontrollable and uncomfortable. I did my research on him, but the answers were limited. I found myself in a trap and could not get out of it...at least, not as easily as I had anticipated.

If you explained to most non-Christian men that you cannot have sexual intercourse with them because it would be fornication, they would ask, "So what else can we do? How, then, do you propose to demonstrate your affection?" Even some Christian men might wonder if you were emotionless.

They might settle for kisses and handholding. In spite of what one learns from the Word of God, one ultimately thinks that taking the next step is a logical step for couples to embrace. Whether we learn this from watching television or previous relationships, it is clear that this learned behavior exists.

Meanwhile, this grown man was not a sixteen-year-old. His expectation was far beyond kisses. *How should I handle this?* I thought to myself. *What exactly should I say? What exactly should I do?* The thoughts raced through my head, raced through my mind.

Remembering that my former boyfriend and I had shared some special moments together despite these limitations, I simply addressed it in a similar manner, naive or unaware of so many things. I had such limited information and knowledge.

Tom's presence was ultimately keeping Dillon in positive behavior. *How can I sever ties with this unbeliever now, when there is so much peace and tranquility in Dillon's life?*

Chapter 11

DESTRUCTIVE PATHS

ONE NIGHT, TOM asked me to meet him at the seaside. He explained that he was feeling ill and that he needed to speak with me.

I was a grown woman who still took up residence at my parents' home, according to custom. I was also a Christian woman who needed to judge or evaluate a situation before entering into it. Considering the time of night, I said, "It's too late. I simply cannot come to you right now. Not so late."

Tom said okay, although I could hear a hint of disappointment in his voice.

If only I could be that adamant with everyone, every time, the Lord would be so pleased. But I have compromised my faith and my principles on various occasions, and in reality, any type of compromise creates problems and results in hurt or anguish.

What is ironic is that one may say "No, thank you," on numerous occasions, but even one small moment of compromise is all the enemy needs to destroy us as believers. For example, although Samson was so strong physically and mentally, one revelation destroyed him completely.

Unfortunately, the world observes us and labels us as hypocrites. Many are clueless to the number of times we have said no.

Nevertheless, Tom did confide in a friend or two about our relationship, and they must have confided in others because their gestures and statements gave it away.

My former boyfriend and I had engaged in such behavior in the past, and it was acceptable with him. Now I needed answers regarding his attitude. I had questions, but more than ever I needed a confidant, a friend, a shoulder to lean on.

Unable to address such matters with family members or my local assembly, I contacted a former boyfriend, who I believed would provide answers without being judgmental. I was candid with him, and he did not judge me. We embraced each other, and I rushed off.

He was not a Christian—he was a religionist. He could not offer scripture verses or pray for my situation. He could only offer his support. The relief I had felt was tremendous. The remarks of others still weighed heavily on my shoulders, but the future seemed hopeful.

Meanwhile, Tom was ready to make his announcement to me that he already had a girlfriend living abroad. I did not see the signs because he always stayed alone—I did not see the signs because I was vulnerable. I did not see the signs; I did not see any signs.

The words, "my wife and my child are returning from abroad tonight," jabbed me like a dagger in my heart. The man who claimed to have no one in his life was now willing to reveal that his heart belonged to another. I said, "I thought you could not have children of your own." "Oh, that's true," he said. Then he alluded, "I have adopted her daughter. She calls me 'Daddy.' She said she needs me to purchase a bike for her. So I need to get her one before meeting them at the airport."

My heart sank even further as I thought to myself,

This man has been saying to me for quite a while that he has no money after paying bills. This man has always acted like a relationship does not need flowers or chocolates. Now he has sufficient funds to purchase a bike and care for a family of three. I was stunned!

He always made excuses not to attend church with me, but now he asked what time my church services begin. He wants his wife and daughter to attend church. The story seemed so surreal. What I heard and saw was a completely different man, one who cared so little about me or the young child, and was fixated on telling lies.

The calls became fewer and fewer until they subsided altogether. He never had an interest in the troubled child's life. He had targeted me all along. *Luckily, I did not consummate our relationship,* I thought to myself a thousand times.

One day, the phone rang. It was Tom.

"How are you?" he asked.

"I'm not sure how to answer that question," I replied.

He repeated the question.

"Did I hurt you?" he asked.

I mumbled something.

"What did you say?" he repeated himself.

I cannot recall whether he said "I'm sorry," but he rambled on. "She told me that she wants to return to the state from which she came."

"Why?" I interrupted, trying to be civil.

"She is bored," he rambled on. "She had a relationship with someone, and she wants to return to him."

I couldn't believe what I was hearing, but I continued to listen.

"The other day she smashed a few glass windows, and I had to call the cops."

"You called the cops, and you *are* a cop?" I responded with a smile on my face.

He doesn't need to be comforted, I told myself. *I know the Word of God says to be kind to your enemies, but I have offered sufficient kindness by listening to his plight.*

Chapter 12

CASTING MY CARES

IT WAS DURING that trying period in my life that I began complaining to almighty God, and He placed a heavy burden within me to write about it. I argued with myself. *Isn't this vindictiveness? This cannot be God.*

At an altar call, God said in His unique way, "I knew what he wanted."

I was now spending quality time with God. Before this series of events, I had never liked to pray. There was a period during which our family conducted family devotions, but we soon became distracted and eventually eliminated the proceedings. I always murmured or complained to myself that prayer was too monotonous, too repetitious. *Do I need to ask for the same things all the time?* Yet, I had kept these thoughts private.

However, it was during that era many years ago, that I received deliverance from habitual sinful actions. I had struggled with sexual desires for so many years. They were periodical, but they still existed. If I fed them enough, they rose up. If I watched sufficient soap operas or feasted on novels that promoted too much lovemaking, the desire was accentuated. Having a non-Christian boyfriend did not rectify or curb the problem either.

On one occasion, I complained to one of my Christian male friends about the neighborhood in which I was raised, and he rebuked me. He said, "I'm from a wealthy neighborhood, and a friend of my mother's taught me a few things. So, living in an under-privileged neighborhood is almost pointless. Human beings are the problem."

His words did offer some level of comfort, but they did not heal or offer deliverance. It was years later that I heard a televangelist candidly express his struggles with the flesh, and that created a sense of normalcy for my struggles. He was a minister who had struggled, yet Jesus did not reject him. He loved the Lord.

For years I have labeled myself as a hypocrite. For years I have asked God why. For years I thought deliverance could never come. I have prayed, and I have fasted. I am trying my best, yet I continuously find myself falling into sin. But God's methods were always different than mine. I love the Lord. I love Christianity. I have seen other lifestyles, but Christianity is all I want, and Jesus is all I need. This is where I want to be; this is where I belong.

Meanwhile I was angry with God. I was enraged with mankind. I was displeased with myself. I blamed the kids. I told God, "If You did not allow me to raise other people's children, I would be doing just fine. Maybe I should have had a few of my own, and the burden would be worth the while," I added.

I loved each of my wards, but at the time I not feel the love. I became verbally abusive to them, telling them that they should be dead. "Maybe I should just end our lives. Your parents would regret their decision. They claim to love you, but they do not really care. They say one thing and do another. They are never present. *I* encountered all the embarrassment. Everyone is promising to assist, and they think that I am blind or foolish. Parents, relatives… they all told me lies. They made promises that they could not keep."

I was beginning to feel suicidal, but I knew that if I acted on that feeling, my faith in God, my family members, and my fellowship assembly would all be affected, so I resorted to prayer.

I used to tell the Lord that He should have allowed Dillon to die when he was a baby. "Look at the kind of dilemma I am involved in because of him." As a baby, he suffered from dehydration. I told the Lord, "You were in charge. Why didn't you take him then? Look at the problems he is causing." If there was not a teacher contacting me, there was an angry principal calling. If a child did not make a complaint, a hostile parent did. It was horrendous! I had no life!

I could not even contemplate marriage, because who would wish for a woman with three children? Certainly not a Christian young man; they usually want children of their own, and I did not want to become a parent at that time. Parenting other people's children can be incredibly challenging.

I lived each day feeling that the children's parents might show up for them. The children also treated me with indifference, telling me bluntly, "You're not my parent." Whenever they experienced any type of illness, I was the one who stayed up late hours and embraced every measure to nurse them back to good health. Their parents were never there. They were never available for their sleepless nights, their pains, their unfinished homework, and all the other issues I had to address. So, I resorted to prayer and complained to God.

There was a time in my life when I was devastated by various situations around me. At night I would listen to the gospel programs introduced in Trinidad by Christian Radio and Margaret Elcock's "Sounds Glorious" program.

As I listened intently to the song lyrics of Donnie McClurkin's "Stand," Kirk Franklin's "My Life Is in Your Hands," the Brooklyn Tabernacle's "Friend of a Wounded Heart" and many others, I experienced gradual but phenomenal transformation in my life.

As I listened to these songs, I was propelled to pray. As I prayed, I also cried, as the song lyrics say. However, prayer was not restricted to nighttime only. I prayed always, I prayed often. I became so close to God that I prayed in the morning, at noontime, and at night, and the pain subsided.

About that period in time, Dr. Myles Munroe began teaching on *Fresh Fire*, a Christian television production that was also founded by Margaret Elcock. He taught about Jeremiah 1:5, "I knew you before you were formed within your mother's womb; before you were born I sanctified you and appointed you as my spokesman to the world (TLB).

Chapter 13

REBUKED BY GOD'S WORDS

I AM UNSURE WHETHER or not the series of events that unfolded after Dr. Myles Munroe altered my way of thinking. What I can attest to is that as Dr. Munroe expounded on Jeremiah 1:5, "Before I formed thee in the belly I knew thee; and before thou camest forth out of the womb I sanctified thee," I observed the profoundness of the scripture verse.

At one point I had the experience of waking up and sobbing early one morning with words uttered in my spirit, *But I guess it's too late to say sorry, Shawn.* Shawn was a nephew, whom death snatched after spending just three brief months on the earth. He was not sick or hurt. He just died.

When he was born, I simply saw him as just another life, another responsibility. After his death, I learned the scripture that says "before the foundation of the world," (Jer. 1:5) and I felt rebuked by God's Words.

I believe that was the first time I heard from the Lord. It was not just the nightmare alone. I could have been on the street walking, seated in a taxi, occupying a restroom, and the tears would well up as a voice in my spirit said, *But I guess it's too late to say sorry, Shawn.*

It occurred so frequently that one day I actually wrote a manuscript about it and labeled it, "Forgive Our Guilt." I was later rebuked for its title, so it is rarely discussed. I knew what had transpired, but it was beyond everyone's comprehension. In addition, the Lord, who had inspired me to write it, gave no green light to publish it.

Months later, someone who I knew consumed a strong substance in order to abort a baby. I knew she had taken matters into her own hand. As I complained about it, the Spirit of God reminded me that I, too, had once persuaded another to consume a beverage that would expedite a menstrual cycle, and I had been wrong.

I had consumed the substance before, and it was effective, but my reason for ingesting the beverage was completely different. However, I, naive of the facts of pregnancy, urged the young lady to drink it quickly, before the formation of her fetus.

Do you remember that group of students who sat beside me at my secondary school? One of them confided that after having intercourse, she took a certain beverage as soon as she missed her menstrual cycle...and it worked every time.

The conversation, however, did not pertain to a menstruation problem; it was an abortion solution. I was too naive to discern its true meaning. After becoming a woman, I had still misjudged the statement. I had unknowingly promoted an abortion.

However, one day in Trinidad, I stumbled upon a container of clean, clear water. In it was a tiny "worm" that, in my estimation, could have been a snake. Unsure of what it really was, I called a relative to verify. I poured a chemical into the water in order to end its life. As soon as the chemical substance touched its body, the creature began to turn and twist in the water. A sharp object was then used to completely mutilate its body.

The manner in which I poured the substance on the

worm, the snake, the creature, reminded me that all life has meaning and value. Therefore it was wrong for me to encourage anyone to consume any type of substance during the initial stages of a pregnancy, thinking that life is too small to have meaning or purpose, because before the foundation...(Jer. 1:5).

The alarming thing was that I immediately remembered what I had encouraged the young woman to indulge in as soon as the final action was completed. I immediately fled the scene, wondering, *Why did this image flash before my eyes?*

Chapter 14

BEARING ANOTHER'S BURDENS

Aftᴇʀ ᴄᴜʟᴍɪɴᴀᴛɪɴɢ "Fᴏʀɢɪᴠᴇ Our Guilt," it was brought to my attention that some believers were falling for the unbelieving community. My knowledge in such matters was so profound that I felt an obligation to my fellow brethren.

I pause to reflect on people whose lives have left an indelible mark on the lives and minds of others, including myself, but no longer serve the King of kings and Lord of lords. These are people whom "the faithful" pass by on a daily basis and probably label them as hopeless. It sometimes becomes easy to say, "They have had their opportunity, it's time to reach out to new souls and usher in new members."

Over the years, I have seen young children born and raised in our assemblies, but the evil one has cunningly tricked them; today they have entered into a Christ-less eternity.

I must prevent others from taking that path or falling completely into that pit, that abyss, I reasoned with myself. I already knew that God wanted me to write about it. He never outlined the approach I should take. Therefore, I generalized.

I addressed parents because too often they are the last ones to know the problems that confront their children. Their offspring obtain information from others that lacks substance or relevancy. Parents need to develop a better rapport with their children.

I addressed pastors because their intentions were good, but their messages kept us thinking that Christianity is only about singing, clapping, and praising God, or maybe about sermons like Jonah in the belly of the fish or maybe the loaves and fishes. Those must be preached because they are the Word of God, but there were real-world situations for which we were totally unprepared. If you lived a protected lifestyle, you barely understood the pressures that the flock was experiencing.

Having endured similar experiences enabled me to confront such topics as the "battle of the mind" in a given situations, topics near and dear to my heart: confessionals, the process, and the return.

I have sinned against almighty God in so many ways, but on one occasion, maybe more, I needed a confessional or confidant before returning home. Once I contacted an ex-boyfriend who was already married. He was the only person to whom I could ask questions when I had no answers. He was the only person in whom I could confide. What alarmed me about that encounter was that an adulterous spirit evidently plagued my life thereafter. I had absolutely no interest whatsoever in men who are already married. I knew that falling in love with them is adultery. But married men were drawn to me. I attracted them and needed deliverance from that adulterous spirit. It was not a spirit that inhabited the body. Rather, it was one that overshadowed my life. As a cloud, I suppose.

People do have legitimate reasons for contesting or obtaining a divorce, but I have seen Christians indulge or embrace the prayer-and-fasting method, and I have seen complete revolution take place.

Consider the parable of the Prodigal Son. In our modern age, many have returned to God because they had been reminded of Psalm 23:6: "And I will dwell in the house of the LORD / Forever" (NKJV). Because many people are reminded of their first love in time, before they self-destruct, I urge the body of Christ to do likewise. Therefore, I write.

Chapter 15

MOVING FORWARD

I HAD OFFICIALLY SAID good-bye to the only man who wanted to take some of the parental burden off my shoulders. It was evident that our children could not co-exist in the same house; our marriage would have ended in a divorce upon commencement.

I loved that Greg loved the Lord with all his heart and that prayer was a factor in all his undertakings, but a marriage was not meant to be. He spent adequate time in prayer over it, and I did too, but there were too many signs pointing in the opposite direction. He did understand me a lot better than most people, but part of me said that it was time to move on. Another part of me wondered if I was making the right decision. Then I remembered what the Lord had revealed to me, and I knew that a dream like that could never be realized with Greg. Consequently, I chose to move on.

I had gained employment at a popular retail outlet. I was moved by the camaraderie of the crew members. Some worked harder than others; some were simply more efficient; some were more experienced. But as all hands pulled together, the very young female supervisor had her mission accomplished daily, weekly, monthly.

Unfortunately, that shift culminated sooner than expected. Meanwhile, the Lord allowed management to be extremely good to me, and they transferred me to another branch. It did take time for me to adjust at my new job, but I came to learn a good deal about retail while serving at the sister company superstore.

It was at that era of my life that I felt the need to join the membership at the Community Christian Center. I had attended sufficient services. The teachings with which I was acquainted seemed similar to some of theirs. The names of three television evangelists with whom I was familiar were reflected there. They were also household names with my late pastor. Seeing one of their names posted in the church's fellowship hall, I felt like I was in familiar territory. I was at home.

Strangely, though, that was not the only reason. On one of my earlier visits to the church years ago, I had attended their all-night prayer meetings, which were awesome. I had never seen that concept implemented before. I knew in my heart that if I would ever have to make a decision later in my life, it could be at the Community Christian Center. Another church also appealed to me and may have been a second choice.

Nevertheless, I had made a decision a long time ago. Therefore, one Sunday morning, I went down to the front row and received membership information. I participated in their classes for the duration. Later, I officially received the Right Hand of Fellowship from both the pastor and his wife and became a member.

My oldest sister, Nora, was present, as well as Bill, a new friend whom I had met after a Sunday morning service. He candidly said that he was not a member. He had been visiting for a while but was undecided. It took me a few years to make the decision as well, so it was difficult for me to judge him.

He was not overly handsome, but he was just about

my age and expressed kindness. We went to the Palisades Mall on the Fourth of July and indulged in a foreign dish. Later, we went by the river to view the fireworks. It was kind of new to me. I thoroughly enjoyed the evening. Finally, Bill took me home and promised to call.

The call came, as did several others. We attended church services together, and he dropped me off at my house afterward. Any time I had the time to spare, we went out. I visited his home one evening after having dinner at a restaurant. We sat, talked, and played gospel music for a while. I looked at his computer and rummaged through his refrigerator. I also spoke with the little child from the next-door apartment before I left.

Not too long after that encounter, our signals began crossing. He would come to my door and ring the bell, and no one would hear it. I would call his number, and he would not be at home. Nothing ran as smoothly as before. The weather was beginning to change as well. Some of my relatives visited me that year, and Bill's schedule and mine could not synchronize, so we went our separate ways.

I later contacted Bill by mail and clarified the confusion. However, as some relatives left, other family matters needed to be addressed; family consumed most of my time. After a couple of months, we drifted apart again and finally went our separate ways.

Chapter 16
DECISIONS

MORE THAN A year had elapsed before Bill suddenly showed up in my driveway. He was driving a different car than the one he had owned previously. Properly attired and wearing a neat haircut, he looked simply stunning.

He came toward the door, but I had already pulled the door open before he could ring the bell. He embraced me and said, "Hi." We went into the dining room where Mother sat. He spoke with her briefly and then asked to speak with me. We went into the living room, and he explained that he needed someone to accompany him to a medical procedure. Mother was having a procedure at another hospital on the same day. I battled with the decision, *should I go with Mother and dismiss him? Or, is this the beginning of something I might regret if I say, "No, thank you"?*

The day finally arrived. The time schedule provided ample time to address Mother's appointment first, and then we were free to drive to the next town. My sister remained with Mother to ensure that her procedure went well. That at least gave me some peace of mind, some sense that I had not abandoned her completely.

Bill did not experience any dizziness after the procedure, so he drove his car. We were to make alternate arrangements if he could not drive. We finished on time and returned to the hospital, where my mother's procedure had also been completed. We all safely returned to our destinations, and I called Bill often to ensure that he was progressing beautifully. Mother needed special attention; we were required to administer medication four times daily for the first week, and the dosage diminished until she was completely healed.

It was not until I needed some assistance with my old computer that Bill paid me a visit. We indulged in some banter afterwards, and, of course, we kissed good night before he headed home.

As time progressed, I simply refused to meet or date another man. I refused to open my heart to anyone else. The little I knew about Bill was fine, I could work around it. Later I realized I was drifting from the standards that God had set; I needed to conduct a series of tests. I said, "I'm not telling anyone else that I am not sexually active." Apparently, everyone—or almost everyone—that I had rebuked or scolded about premarital sex or involvement in non-Christian relationships eventually got married.

I told the Lord, "The next time anyone shows up with just a hint of interest in me, I'm giving myself completely to him. You obviously bless people like that anyway. Why am I trying so hard to be an advocate for righteousness? I am still single, and they are not."

I added, "Well, this time I am going to consummate the union." He could have had a disease, but that was the last thought on my mind. He did not promise that we would get married or engaged, but I was determined to go a step further.

Despite how I felt, I kept listening to Christian programming. Gradually my mind began to change as one minister's favorite message was fornication. Another female pastor said something striking about "churchgoers who are not necessarily Christians," and that had me wondering whether Bill was just a "churchgoer." It had crossed my mind before. My pastors from the Community Christian Center as well as my former ministers had preached frequently on fornication. So, the instruction was sufficient.

I tried to show Bill a scripture verse in 1 Corinthians 10 regarding premarital sex, but he blatantly refused to read it. He knew that I had previously underlined one of those verses in his Bible.

Meanwhile, my pastor, Pastor Jane, from the Community Christian Center had called my house to wish me a happy birthday from both her and her husband, and I was consumed with elation. I bragged about it to everyone who had forgotten my birthday that year (usually I get a barrage of calls, but I did not receive many that year). That one special call from my pastor bore much significance, although she did not know it.

The day had arrived for Bill and me to celebrate my birthday, and all I could think of was my pastor's phone call. I had fasted weeks before, asking God to make plain His thoughts regarding Bill and me.

Bill called me, and although I had prepared my clothing to go out with him, I told him that I felt ill. He could not believe it, so he asked if he should come over to my house. I answered yes because I really did suffer from visible symptoms, and he could determine that I was in bad shape. It was not bad enough, but it was sufficient for him to understand that I really felt unwell.

Bill looked me straight in the eye and asked, "When did you change your mind?" My heart sank. I was astounded; he knew exactly what I was thinking.

"I told you, I am not feeling well." I asked, "Can't you

see I am coughing constantly?" He repeated the question adamantly. "I asked you, how long ago did you change your mind?"

I answered, "Sometime this evening." He gave me a long, hard, cold stare as he allowed his finger to glide across his lips, from side to side, from one end to the other. Very slowly, he repeated the process. I reached out to him almost immediately, assuring him that I really cared, but it was impossible for us to go anywhere that night. Yet in a heartbeat, petting occurred, and I displeased God.

I repented. Only the Lord knew what my heart truly reflected. The Lord already knew my past remarks.

In reality, I have tried to walk uprightly, circumspectly before God. Whenever I met anyone, I kept thinking that this one might take my hand in marriage, but it never happened. I was never too anxious about being married. I just did not wish to hurt God and fall into sin. Therefore, marriage was the only way out, the only way of escape. When it did not occur in my twenties, I felt that the Lord saw my immaturity and was not ready to bless me with a husband. It did not occur in my thirties either, because there was always another woman lurking in the shadows somewhere. I have prayed. I have fasted. I have been unsure how to handle this situation. Now I am a grown, unmarried woman.

Bill and I went to the movies after that encounter. Maybe several weeks had passed, but the mission had already been accomplished. The devil got me exactly where he wanted me. One sinful moment was all he required. We did not consummate the union on that day either, although Bill had expectations. The entire evening was filled with mixed emotions. It felt more like the beginning of the end, and it was. Shortly afterward, the relationship was terminated.

Realizing that we would not be consummating our union that night either, Bill uttered to himself very softly, "I have never met anyone like you before." I gave no response but immediately said to myself, "You were sent!"

To reiterate an earlier remark, I had experienced moral failures before. I was angry with almighty God. Maybe deep within, I really blamed Him. I was infuriated with everyone who possessed even a hint of information about my sin. I was furious about the children that God had allowed into my life. Today, ten years later, almost the exact behavior has resurfaced. I cannot comprehend how almighty God–the God of Omnipotence, God of Omniscience, and the Omnipresent God–would require me to write about sin, knowing that I would face a recurrence.

I allege that on one occasion, a church member informed my pastor. At this time, the Lord told me plainly that He was not going to reveal it. He said, "I am not going to reveal it, you are." Then He showed me my hypocrisy through the scriptures in Romans 2. He allowed me to hear several ministers preach about repentance, and He ministered to my spirit.

One day I asked, "How do I know it's you? It could be my conscience speaking. Therefore," I said to the Lord, "if I go to the volunteer coordinator tomorrow at church, and she asks just one question pertaining to those events, I shall know it's You who has spoken."

Before leaving I argued again. "But Lord, it is a church where You reveal things prophetically. You can reveal it."

No sooner had I arrived than Mrs. Peters said, "Sit down. What's going on? Talk to me."

"I am here to volunteer. We can talk when I have finished," I suggested. There was no animosity between us. We both spoke calmly. She insisted that we talk first. I glanced at my pocketbook, which lay beside me. Then I turned toward her and said, "I have had a moral failure."

She probed into the story, asking, "What was it? Was it 'oral'?"

"No."

"Was it intercourse?"

"No."

"What was it?" she insisted.

I felt my spirit plunge within me as I said, "I just think that I went too far."

She surrendered by saying, "If you need counseling, that's for Pastor Jane."

I already knew how embarrassing and humiliating that could be. Her husband had just passed away, and the last thing that she needed was news about inappropriate behavior from her church members. The Lord had placed her in authority, as head of the church, and He had said that I needed to reveal it, so I obeyed. I decided to tell her that I had sinned without embellishing the facts.

It was a Wednesday night. She was not expecting this. I wanted to get it over, once and for all. It took a great deal of courage to approach her. As I uttered the words, "moral failure," I was hoping to receive a rose for my honesty, but it was not meant to be. She said calmly, "Call me tomorrow," and the saga began.

The Lord wanted to walk me through this gradually, step by step, stage by stage. As soon as I completed a letter of apology and explanation, I waited for more of

God's instructions because He was dealing with me separately. Letter by letter, I wrote about my sin. "My sin entailed…"

Another one read, "I forgot to mention the young man's name."

I felt her pain, her anguish. I felt the weight of pastoring on her shoulder. I had seen the difficulty of dealing with out-of-control members in the past, and it troubled me sorely, bitterly.

I wish I could say that it took mere days, weeks, or months for the Lord to relieve me from my punishment, but in actuality, it took years.

Chapter 17
PAYING A PRICE

IT IS NOTABLE that my sin had entangled various aspects of my life as well as the lives of family members. A good deal of money had been wasted before my confessions. It is said that we always pay a price. I have paid a high price—a huge price—for this sin. It is also notable that each time I wrote a letter to Pastor Jane, some form of deliverance came.

I urgently needed to acquire some legal documents. I spent money for an entire year, and saw no positive results. After my confessions, what I had attempted the previous year was finalized. I was required to pay the same fees, but there was expedition as well as victory after the confessions. Strongholds and walls promptly came down.

I have learned that the Lord God works differently in each circumstance. He is not a stereotypical god. Sometimes deliverance comes through repentance or confessions to just anyone. Sometimes it comes through prayer and fasting, through financial giving and offerings, through altar calls, or simply through confession to God alone. In this case, the confessions to my pastor brought about the positive change. God even expected me to reveal the young man's name and true identity.

Whenever we sin, we open doors to the devil, the enemy of our souls. Ordinarily, he has no access into our lives. He cannot infiltrate our space without our permission. He obviously releases all types of spirits, and these can become evident through joblessness, sickness, diseases, financial hardships, or even death. James 5:16 says, "Confess your faults one to another…that ye may be healed."

Therefore, confessions to pastors are sometimes necessary in order to realize change, deliverance, or restoration. I cannot promise that your pastor will pat you on the back. It *is* sin that I am referring to.

If you need someone's prayers to be answered, just confess your fault to one another, such as your pastors or congregation, for positive changes to be realized. Remember, righteousness exalts, but sin is a reproach (Prov. 14:34, NKJV).

God is a god of order. The church also calls for order and discipline; the world demands it. So we need to humble ourselves, which is not easy to do, but our heavenly Father is always well pleased when we do.

Chapter 18

CHRISTIAN GIRL TALK

THE PASTOR AND staff of the Community Christian Center of New York had planned on teaching its membership about appropriate Christian behavior. The announcement read, "Attention, Ladies! Pastor Jane will be having a 'Serious Christian Girl Talk' here on Saturday, September 10 at 10:00 a.m. Bring your Bible, a concordance, pen, paper, and a willingness to be honest before the Lord."

I felt I knew exactly where that was stemming from, and I was not entirely thrilled about attending. Although of course I loved the Lord, not all churches know how to deal with sin among their membership. One girl reported that she had a mental breakdown after confessing her faults to her pastor. She eventually changed her membership.

Because the Lord was also dealing with me, I, too, had a nightmare of being in rough and choppy waters up to my neck, and I tried to swim out of it. Because the dream occurred on a Sunday morning, I decided, "I'm not attending church today." Nevertheless, ministers must get the job done, regardless of how their followers feel.

According to 2 Timothy 3:16–17, "All scripture is given by inspiration of God, and is profitable for doctrine, for reproof, for correction, for instruction in righteousness:

That the man of God may be perfect, thoroughly furnished unto all good works."

Despite how I felt, I attended the prayer meeting on the Friday night prior to the talk, and the announcer did encourage the ladies to support the following day's session. Various people spoke, and I finally got the message. I have attended numerous sessions like these before. Although there were similarities among them, each was a unique learning experience.

Nevertheless, at this session, I received the answers that I had needed for most of my life. I had heard many versions before, but I never made a connection. One thing seemed to have nothing to do with the other.

Again I reminisced, pondering, *Why was this revealed now, and at this Christian Center? Was the Lord planning some special project for this church?* He had given me a command long before I even knew the location of the church. I knew it existed, because I had relatives who were once members. Before joining I had no idea that I would one day become a member. I also knew that it was a church known for hearing from God prophetically, and I knew that it would be similar to the one in which I worshipped during my early years.

The session lasted from ten o'clock in the morning until five o'clock in the evening. I still needed answers, but those would come directly from the Lord in His time. However, I had ample time to think, to ponder the sessions' usefulness. I later decided to document my thoughts, resulting in the writing of *Drifted*.

I stared my sin in the face and wondered, *Was it the result of the exposure I had in my childhood?* I no longer had any struggles with certain desires; Jesus had delivered me through transparency over a decade ago. Am I eager to be married? Sometimes I am, but other times I am not keen on the idea. It is the way God has made us, but on many occasions I simply was not seeking to find anyone.

The church teaches that fornication and adultery are sin. It is taught that fornication is sexual intercourse with an unmarried person. I have convinced myself for years that the intercourse itself is sin. Yet, there is something in each of us that tells us when we have done wrong.

When I had struggles with sexual desires, I prayed and fasted, but the problem was never eradicated. I have never been counseled, although that might not have worked either. It was pointed out that masturbation is having sex with oneself, and it is wrong. It was also hinted that watching those steamy reality shows on television and then having sex with one's own husband is also wrong. I was just thrilled that I was not experiencing those challenges during the church teachings.

Now, whenever your male friends teach you that petting is something that people do when they love each other, they are actually preparing you for intercourse. Some people may or may not suggest that they are simply seeking pleasure or gratification. Either they are trying to entrap you, or they lack knowledge. Pastor Jane also strongly condemns kissing, although it is viewed as a typical or acceptable behavior in relationships. She even denounces the holding of hands.

A deacon at the Community Christian Center described petting as a preparation for sex. He said, "It is like playing baseball, where there is a first base, second base, third base, sometimes fourth base, and home." Kissing, I recall, was referred to as first base. Where or when do our church members obtain such information? Is it at marriage counseling, lectures, or discussions? Or is it from reading explicit books? Does the church encourage its followers to read or indulge in such explicit material?

Do you see why there is so much ignorance among the body of Christ? Remember the Bible says, "Where there is no vision, the people perish..." (Prov. 29:18). So many people were born into the church and never married or received any form of counseling. Consequently, the enemy, fully ahead of the game, exposes us to sex in our childhood, and to lovemaking as teenagers. By the time we are ready to be married, we have learned the first step last and the last step first. Children do not think that far ahead.

Would we become great marriage partners? Or is this a recipe for a disastrous relationship? Is this one reason for the high divorce rate in our churches?

I have nothing against people who are divorced; it is necessary at times. Nevertheless, the church experiences sexual problems, and those who struggle are silent. They are fearful of being shunned, derided or vilified. So they occupy our pews in pretense.

If many believers were to confess their sins to their pastors, the church would become very effective according to 2 Chronicles 7:14, which states, "If my people, which are called by my name, shall humble themselves, and pray, and seek my face, and turn from their wicked ways; then will I hear from heaven, and will forgive their sin, and will heal their land."

However, most ministers detest hearing that they have sin in their camp. Therefore, the congregation, who loves the Lord wholeheartedly but has struggles, remains silent. Homosexuality sometimes starts in childhood, not adulthood. How, then, can this curse be reversed? Many of us do not know how to seek God for simple things. How would we have the knowledge or solution to other problems? In addition, we claim to love the Lord on one hand and drift into many sinful practices on the other. Can transparency affect change?

Whenever we begin to view sin as a murdered body that lies dormant at the bottom of the ocean, only one that can eventually resurface, we will act differently. We alter our behaviors drastically because we remember that our sin will find us out.

The Serious Christian Girl Talk was biblically and brilliantly executed!

Chapter 19
AN OLD POLICY

O<small>N A FEW</small> occasions I have adopted a policy of indulging in prayer and fasting to determine what God was trying to tell me about my relationships with men. As I indicated previously, I had embarked upon the same practice with Bill. On two occasions, I refused to inform him of my whereabouts. I left messages telling him not to worry because I was just taking some time off. I knew that could be interpreted in various ways, but it was a chance I needed to take.

I knew I was beginning to love Bill, and I was obligated to find out whether or not I was treading dangerous ground. God should have taken preeminence in my life, but I was drifting–drifting badly.

I have no recollection of the purpose of the first fast, but on the second occasion, I told the Lord that this was the second encounter Bill and I were having, and I wished to hear from Him. "It is imperative," I told the Lord, "If You're involved, make it plain. If You are not, make it clear." I also desired a new job and supposed that would be part of the sign.

There must have been unconfessed sin in my life because I had barely completed the fast when I received a telephone call. A familiar voice was at the end of the line. It was a businessman named Mr. Bud, an entrepreneur with whom I had previously worked. "A client of mine," he reported, "is very ill and needs any kind of assistance you can offer." He added, "I know your ability, and I believe you can help."

A day or two must have passed, and I went to assist the woman. She needed an aide. She needed a doctor. She needed movers. She needed help urgently. Mrs. Dee was a tall, beautiful, kindhearted, soft-spoken, red-haired, Caucasian woman. She had once been wealthy, as she had owned a business with her late husband, whom I never met.

She belonged to a cult, and each morning she would awake and play the tape of the late founder of her faith. I offered my assistance in every way I could; I packed items from her room and itemized and properly labeled each box for storage. She would require a new home. Her friends brought her cooked food, and all she was required to do was reheat the food.

A good deal of work was completed before the realtors arrived. She asked that I open the door and direct them to the room where she sat. I then returned to work.

She had signed some documents to the bank, which was in charge of her house. She was too ill to work. She had no husband to offer her assistance, and she could no longer pay the note for the property. Her income was simply insufficient to meet her demands.

The following day, Mrs. Dee's condition worsened. She was too ill to get out of bed. She had no home and no relatives. She was an only child; her husband was an only child. They had neither children nor siblings.

I worked with her that day, clearing her chest of drawers and closet and labeling boxes of items that she might need in her new home—an apartment, maybe. A studio was too small for the number of items she wanted

An Old Policy

to keep. Some of her possessions would need to be sold. Her piano and many other valuables would give her an adequate sum of money for storage and personal use.

A neighbor offered her a room, but her possessions were far too many to take there. Besides, she was now too ill to reside at her neighbor's house. She did not believe in doctors, according to her faith or religion.

That was the last day I saw Mrs. Dee. I returned to work the following Monday. She was boarding with her scientology family. They owned a facility that housed patients, and Mr. Bud had negotiated with them. They could pray for her whenever it was necessary, according to their teachings, and friends were free to visit.

I spoke with her on the telephone on a few occasions. I always tried to make her laugh. *That's good medicine*, I thought. *She's already inundated with debts.* I shared my faith in Jesus Christ with her, but it was the first time I had heard of her religion. She was clever in conveying the information sparingly. One day, I told her on the phone, "Just speak to Jesus." She did say, "Yes, you're right. You're right." That was our final conversation.

The bank wanted the house on a particular day. Mr. Bud's wife and all other workers were required to quicken the pace. She did say on a few occasions that I was free to take anything that I really wanted, because I was such a great help. Each room became more than we could handle, more than we could consume.

The week was finally ending. She already requested to set aside a specific pantsuit, "should something happen," she said. I obeyed the request, but I did not ask for what use. The businessman made storage arrangements while his wife and I cleared any documents she might need from her car. The house was officially released over to the bank that Friday. The car was returned to the leasing company the following Monday. Mrs. Dee passed away on Tuesday.

Mr. Bud's wife called the very next night to inform me, but I knew all along that Mrs. Dee was saying goodbye. Mrs. Bud was named executor at Mrs. Dee's request. She finalized the funeral proceedings, and just neighbors, friends, and acquaintances attended.

Remember those gifts that I was privileged to take from Ms. Dee? I cannot tell whether spirits were transferred, but several weeks later I noticed that similar attacks began to invade my home. When a home is under attack by these forces, sometimes confessing sin is imperative to reformation; sometimes it requires expulsion. I have seen such forces permeate the atmosphere in the past. I do know that I fasted and prayed with my sinful body. I know now that forces can enter homes and lives through adultery, fornication, and every other form of sexual activity. I am also confident that some do inhabit or possess the human body through intercourse.

The enemy knows that sexual sin is far more than we can fathom in our own power. Therefore, the angel of light camouflages sin and throws it into the pathway of the believer. This is one area in which he evidently desires to sift us as wheat or shatter us to pieces, and is sometimes able to do so. Therefore, he plays games with our emotions or minds. He allows people to speak certain words that will ultimately affect our thoughts and emotions. He puts us into compromising positions; then he strikes. Do you see the deception in the snake, the angel of light, the devil, Satan? I once heard minister Charles Stanley refer to sexual sins as "landmines in the pathway of the believer."

Chapter 20
FACT-FINDING MISSION

HAVING PORTRAYED MYSELF as a woman who thrives only on flirtatious behavior, I reflect on the occasions when only almighty God knew the truth. Times when I blatantly refused to get into a vehicle with men for whom I cared or who professed to care for me. There were moments when I would overdress myself to discourage any type of violation or inappropriateness. There were moments in which I would avoid taking telephone calls in an effort to maintain my salvation and walk with the Lord.

There were indeed persistent individuals who sought only my demise. They arrived in disguise, but their true intent was disclosed so that my heavenly Father's name would not be smeared.

Still, I cannot take all the praise for effort, as the Holy Spirit would lead me along a plain path on many occasions. He would send an angel to deliver me from being raped because "The angel of the LORD encampeth round about them that fear him, and delivereth them" (Ps. 34:7).

Indeed, it is a journey, because celibacy wears many faces. No one who takes a vow of abstinence reaches a ripe old age without purposing in his heart, like Daniel, that he would not defile himself (Dan. 1:8).

Only the Holy Spirit, whose purpose is to observe and prove all things, knows the conversations between couples. Only Jesus can give an eyewitness account of time. The only time I had to send my wards to different locations was so that I could entreat God and assume my authority as a believer, recognizing that the evil one desired to sift me as wheat.

Still, plagued by numerous questions, I decided to pursue a fact-finding mission:

> *Having overcome so many obstacles, why am I still falling into sin?*
>
> *Why would the God of omniscience ask me to write about topics for which I have so few answers?*
>
> *Why would God observe sheer decadence in my life and delegate such a responsibility?*
>
> *Why would He call me faithful in 1999, when He knew that I would repeat an inappropriate behavior?*
>
> *Was God saying that I would be faithful to my charge?*
>
> *Why am I still wondering how to free myself from men who are already married to other women?*

I concluded that almighty God would provide answers in His time or season. Nevertheless, the following information, in my estimation, needs to be documented.

I did express flirtatiousness at times, and I compromised my faith on many occasions. My expressions of loyalty to men were obviously more than those I offered to almighty God.

The Lord also expects me to compare and improve the wording of my script, "Fallen for the Unbeliever." All inappropriate behavior is upsetting to God. Every stage or phase of petting is intolerable. God has designed cuddling, lovemaking, kissing, and every other act for marriage, and it culminates in the marital bed. Whenever any of the aforementioned behaviors are executed by born-again believers, God labels them as married.

In "Fallen," confessions were portrayed as embarrassing to the believer. The Lord has taken me through so many stages that I now believe public confessions to a pastor, or maybe the congregation, are imperative after sin. Healing and deliverance can be realized from them. Failure to observe confessionals can result in death.

Any type of inappropriate behavior creates an opportunity for the enemy to enter into your finances and create homelessness for you and your relatives, or poverty from joblessness. The Lord wanted me to know that I cannot conquer what I do not confront. The enemy obviously detected that I was not fully delivered from the pleasures that endured for a season, and he periodically presented them to me on different platters over a considerable period of time. I have also discovered that none of the men who claimed to love me really loved me as much as I thought. Therefore, my heavenly Father shielded and comforted me from any violators.

The Lord also wanted to remind me that without godliness, no man will see God. I must always seek to remember that sin is the breaking of God's Word and Law. It is any word, thought, or action that comes between God and me.

In addition, I have gained new appreciation from the verse, "God is light, and in Him is no darkness at all" (1 John 1:5).

Chapter 21

ONE FINAL THOUGHT

SISTERS AND BRETHREN, I would be filled with regret if I left you without hope. The God we serve is all-powerful. He remains Creator of the Universe. He remains Healer and Deliverer of Humankind. I have seen His operation over the years, and I have proven that He is real!

However, it is beyond me to reveal why some have never received their healing or even have never married. Personally, I do not think that I persevered in the same manner as some of my fellow Christians who are married. The longing for marriage once existed in me, but I never engaged in the same measure of prayer that some of my friends did. I continue to support blissful marriages because God initiated marriage. I still wish to be married, but the overwhelming sense of longing has subsided.

While I stand steadfast and wait for God's ultimate plan to unfold, I choose to occupy myself in matters pertaining to the Lord. Over a decade ago, I drew nigh to almighty God after I sinned against Him. One Sunday, I was at an altar call because everyone was asked to come forward. I was raising three children then, and a woman of God asked me what I wanted her to pray for me. I said, "I am fine. I simply need to know what God wants me to do with the children in my care." The woman of God smiled. Then she asked that I raise my hand in prayer before God. She continued, "What do you think the Lord wants you to do for Him?"

Because the Lord was not very specific, I kept hoping that His servant would reveal the answer to me. But the God we serve is so different from humankind. Instead, the woman of God instantly stopped praying and said, "But you know already."

Now that I fully comprehend what the Lord was requesting, I expect to reveal the degree of ambivalence that exists among believers, both young and old. God did not intend to speak only to me; He also wanted to speak to you. And in my humble way, I shared those revelations with you through the pages of the book, *Drifted*.

ABOUT THE AUTHOR

SHEVON FREDERICK HAS spent many years working as an Early Childhood educator. Her involvement in numerous committees and groups is reflective in Christian education, sports, politics and drug prevention groups. She was once a member of the Westchester Christian Writers Workshop in New York.

Shevon loves reading, poetry, traveling, listing to gospel music and viewing various sporting activities. Although she has discovered a hidden passion for the retail industry, teaching and working with young children yield more benefits for her.

The author resides in Rockland County, New York.

CONTACT THE AUTHOR

Shevon Frederick

P.O. Box 878

Spring Valley, NY 10977-9998

(845) 425-8185

www.shevonfrederick.com

www.ingramcontent.com/pod-product-compliance
Lightning Source LLC
LaVergne TN
LVHW021400080426
835508LV00020B/2384